# Heaven Forbid!

## Bible Skits

### with the

## Human Touch

**Leon Doolin**
**Illustrated by Mark Redford**

Library of Congress Catalog Card Number: 95-62285

ISBN 0-9650207-4-6

*Dedicated to My Wonderful Family:*

*My wife, Geraldine, and my children,
Angela and Melissa*

# TABLE OF CONTENTS

# FOREWORD

The Bible is in many homes, and yes, in our places of worship, setting on shelves gathering dust. The purpose of this book isn't to hypothesize all the reasons for laying this great road map of the Judeo Christian faith aside. But, through the ministry of drama, it's hoped that it's relevancy to us in the 20th, and soon approaching 21st century, can be brought to life.

First of all, the Thee's, Thou's, and Thine, terms from the Kings English that has discouraged folks from reading the Bible need not be a hurdle. Many new translations of the Bible puts the words into today's English. The use of drama skits involving our own words that we most easily understand can further break down the semantic wall.

Secondly, even though the setting in which great events of the Bible took place is an important element in the stories' accounts, transforming many of these events into a setting we can more readily identify with can help us in applying *great* Biblical truths in our modern day society. Through the drama skits in this book, these events are placed in today's settings.

Thirdly, we may find it very difficult to relate to the people in the Bible. They may very well be perceived by us as supernatural beings, great heroes of the faith that we might only relate to in our farthest dreams. And, even though there is plenty of evidence in scripture of many of their weaknesses, which point out the fact that they were human, we see only the final outcome, an unwavering faith, even death for the cause of Christ. Admittedly, the Bible does not include every moment of doubt, the questioning of God's will, of not having the greatest faith at all times. Yet, without detracting from these great Biblical character's heroism, we need to affirm them as fellow human beings, having been given, as we, a portion of faith, perhaps no larger than a grain of mustard seed. And, with that little bit of faith, the people we read about applied it towards better understanding their God.

So, in the drama skits, we read between the lines, so to speak, without adding to or taking from the Bible stories' intent. We bring out individuals' humanness, we witness their struggles to attain their victories.

As many of the skits are performed, their flavor tends to take on the humorous side of life. But, this isn't all bad. Think of the many times we can look back at some of our own previous struggles with a hearty laugh or two. As we laugh throughout the skits, we can witness God's hand leading those humans in supernatural ways and affirm His power working through us today.

It is my hope that you will catch the "drama skit BUG" as you participate in these skits and that this book will be a springboard for your continued development of Biblical drama and the unfolding of God's Word, the Bible.

Leon Doolin

# ACKNOWLEDGEMENTS

A SPECIAL THANKS TO THE FOLLOWING PEOPLE
WHO ENCOURAGED AND ASSISTED IN MAKING THIS
BOOK A REALITY:

To Melanie Walls and Art Oswalt
　　for their encouragement and support

To Betty Anne Fry and Marilyn Valuet
　　for help in typing the manuscript

To Vivian Bradbury of Sans Serif
　　for her patience and special touches

To Christine Blanke of Thomson-Shore Book
　　Manufacturing for her patience, time and
　　suggestions

To Victory Ministries as acting publisher
　　and supporter

To Mark Redford
　　For illustrating the book

# I

# INTRODUCTION
## Laying the Groundwork

# PICTURE THIS

◆ ◆ ◆

It's a typical evening Lenten program at a small church perhaps even yours, with the exception of one thing. Tonight, there are 60 people gathered. There are usually 26–28 assembled for these Lenten programs. The Education Committee is hosting tonight's soup and sandwich entree. Each committee represented in the church takes a turn hosting an evening. That means several committee members bring their favorite pot of soup or stew and others contribute the cheeses, crackers and other finger foods to add to the meal. Everyone who comes out for the evening program is responsible for bringing his or her sandwich. Usually there is a video

3

presented, a guest speaker or concert performed.

So, what is the reason for a bigger crowd tonight? Could it be a special soup that will be served? It's funny no one seems to know anything about the soups except the people who are contributing them. Five people know they are involved in a drama skit as part of the program. But is it the skit that is the draw of tonight's crowd? It can't be so. Hardly anyone seems to know that these people are participating in any way except, perhaps, their own immediate families.

After the meal, a program leader steps forward and asks the audience to keep the aisles clear. "There may be some action in the aisles tonight," he cautions those gathered. The five people look at each other and at the person in charge in bewilderment as if to say, "What's this all about? We won't be using any aisles. Our little skit will take place in a small area in the corner of the room."

A short prayer is offered for His guidance in the program. Following the prayer, three people come forward and seat themselves at the front of the sanctuary. Several youngsters rush up to them with mirrors, hairbrushes, combs and make-up to take care of last minute touchups. A camera crew comes

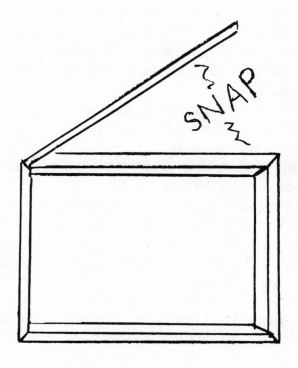

*Figure 1.    The slate.*
*It is easy to construct using small*
*pieces of 1' × 2' wood. The center could*
*be made of cardboard or a small piece*
*of paneling material. The small piece*
*of wood that 'SNAPS' is attached at*
*one end by a small hinge.*

in loaded to the hilt with headphone sets, recorders, video cameras, etc. In a couple of seconds, special lighting is in place and a crewman calls out, "Ready on the set." Next, a young person comes forward with a "slate" (see Figure 1), gives it a snap and says, "Ready, take 5."

"Welcome to tonight's Jan Butler Show," announces the talk show hostess. "Tonight we'll be addressing the concerns of parents having children in their very late years. Our guests are two couples who through special intervention were able to bear children in their very old age. Please welcome our two couples, Abraham and Sarah, parents of Isaac, and Elizabeth and Zacharias, parents of John the Baptist . . ."

As the evening progresses, the five people realize that they are not the only participants tonight. The first one, "The Jan Butler Show," and theirs, "The Return of the Prodigal Son," are only two of five skits that will be presented. The surprising element of the program is that no less than 45 of the people present tonight are actively involved in one or more of the skits!

What is also intriguing about this area of ministry is that those who are regular participants approach new reluctant people with the reassurance that they, too, can do it. As these people attain some level of comfort in "doing something up front," they acquire the confidence, then, to serve in various other roles in the church requiring them to be up front speaking.

The greatest satisfaction comes, however, when individuals come up to the drama director after the evening's program proclaiming their new interest and enlightenment of particular aspects of the Bible.

# THE FORMAT AND SETTING

◆ ◆ ◆

The skits in this book tend to lend themselves to fitting into specific formats, as described below:

1. The TV newscast on-the-spot interview as in the skits, "Noah and the Ark," and "The Taking of Jericho." No actual backdrop or scenery is needed. It is all in our imagination. The main prop is the news reporter's earphone set and portable microphone.

2. A TV talk show, as mentioned previously, with a talk show host and a line up of guests discussing a specific topic such as Raising Chil-

dren as Elderly Parents, with guests Abraham and Sarah/ Zacharias and Elizabeth. The front of the room is done up as a TV talk show set with seats for the host and guests. (A table for the host is optional.) A camera crew on the side of the set lends a feeling of authenticity to this setting.

3.  A scripted skit with participants acting. Real or imaginary props add to the skit's interpretation. Usually a backdrop or specific scenery is not necessary. An example of such a skit is "The True God Contest" on page 43.

4.  The same as #3 except one or two narrators read the script as performers with specific roles act out (pantomime) what is being read.

5.  The monologue can be, but not limited to, an individual speaking as a particular Bible personality. See "The Monologue."

The format you use to tell the story will depend on which you deem the most comfortable one for you (not necessarily the formats selected as examples in this book), and the one which you feel is the best for getting the message across. But, some Bible stories tend to lend themselves more to one format than another. Once you get into analyzing these stories from a drama standpoint, you will develop a feel for the most suitable format.

# BEGINNING AND ENDING THE SKITS

◆ ◆ ◆

Instead of the usual, "This is a skit about . . ." to begin a skit or saying, "The End" to terminate a skit, the following are other suggested ways to lead into the skits and to exit them.

For the "News Cast" skits such as "Noah and the Ark" and "The Taking of Jericho," having a news anchor person in the news room introduce the reporter in the field and the news breaking story is a creative approach to starting off this type of skit. The reporter then would take over with the interview.

A suitable ending to the above mentioned type of skits would be for the reporter, following the interview, to take the audience back to the anchor desk where the anchor person might say something like:

> "Thank you, (name of reporter) for that news breaking story. We'll be informing you (the viewing audience) as to any further happenings in this story as it continues to unfold."

You may wish, as the news anchor person, to give an update on the event later in your news cast skit.

Another suitable ending to a news cast story would be for the reporter to take the audience back to the anchor person who might say something like:

> "We now take you by satellite to the next news story of the evening . . ." (If another news cast skit is to follow).

An example of a "lead in" for a talk show is provided in the beginning chapter of this book. The use of a TV camera crew, the make-up crew and the host(ess) announcing the subject of the show should captivate the audience and set the tone for what is about to happen.

An appropriate ending to the talk show would be a brief summary offered by the talk show host(ess) and a conclusive statement stemming from the interview. He or she might then invite the audience to stay tuned to next week's show where _____ will be the topic of discussion.

For any of the Bible skits that are read while being pantomimed, the reader may wish to begin the skit by visually (before the audience) opening a large book or folder while saying one of the following:

1. "Now hear the Word of the Lord taken from (Bible reference) . . ."
2. "The Friend at Midnight" (Simply stating the title)

To end this type of skit, the reader may want to visually close the book or folder while saying one of the following:

1. "Thus ends the story (parable) of _____"
2. "Now, let him who has ears to hear (pause as he or she places hand at back of ear) acknowledge what the Word of the Lord has said."

## Introduction

To introduce a person who is going to do a monologue, invite the individual to the front of the auditorium as one would a guest speaker. Little otherwise needs to be said in the way of introduction since most of who or "what" they are to represent should come out in the monologue.

It is most appropriate for the person doing the monologue to conclude it himself. An informal, "Oh how time flies. I must be going," or something similar would provide a smooth and natural ending.

A scripted play or skit should be introduced formally as such. The emcee should introduce the play by name and tell what group (Youth, seniors, drama club, etc.) is performing. A brief statement about the performers as a group might add interest to the audience. If the play is Biblically based, as the ones in this book are, the emcee should also introduce the scripture reference from which the play is based.

The ending to the play is evident by all the players exiting the stage or other performance area. They may or may not wish to come out to take a bow. But, it would be most appropriate for them to come back out on the floor to be introduced. The emcee may do this or a designee from among the players may do the honors.

## Beginning and Ending the Skits

Creative beginnings and endings should add to smoother transitions between the skits, help hold the audience's attention, and provide some humor and interesting role-playing for participants.

# II

# SOME SHORT BUT POWER-PACKED PARABLES

# THE LOST COIN
# A Parable

◆ ◆ ◆

*Scripture background: Luke 15:8-10*
*Cast of Characters:*
    *Narrator*
    *Owner of the lost coin*
    *Searchers of the coin—4–10 children*

This skit is great for younger children, ages 4-6. The scriptural text could be used for this skit but it would almost be ended before the children could get into it. The story written below and read by a narrator (or told by a

19

narrator) could make it more interesting for the children:

> The Kingdom of Heaven is so important that it is just like a person who had a very valuable coin. But one day the coin came up missing. The owner of this coin began looking everywhere for the missing coin. He (she) looked under rugs, between books, around dishes and other things throughout the house. He (she) even went outside to look for the coin but was unable to find it. He (she) was so sad that the neighbors came over to see what was the matter. Then they, too, joined in the search for the lost coin. They looked throughout the morning hours, through the noontime, not even stopping for lunch, and into the evening hours when it became dark outside. Many other things were found throughout the day but not the coin. Then suddenly . . . Wait a minute . . . It can't be. But there it was. Even in the darkness of the night, the coin was found.
>
> Everyone was so glad the coin was found that they joined in together in celebration. This is how

valuable the Kingdom of God is. The End.

Suggestions for making this skit meaningful: The person who has lost the coin needs to convey the "feeling of having experienced a great loss" to the audience. Perhaps you, as the director, can help this child by having him think of something very important that he may have lost, and their feelings and emotions that surfaced at that time.

Also, it would be a good idea to have odds and ends "planted" for all the searchers to pick up to create a type of treasure hunt for them.

Lastly, there needs to be a specific child selected ahead of time to be the one who finds the coin. Allowing other children in on this information before the skit could offset some false expectancy about them being the coin finder. Also, it should be emphasized that the excitement over the lost coin surfacing is to be shared among everyone! Everyone joins hands and jumps up and down for joy!

# THE PHARISEE
# AND THE PUBLICAN

◆ ◆ ◆

*Scriptural background: Luke 18:9–14*
*Cast of Characters:*
*    Narrator (Reader)*
*    Pharisee and Publican (Ages 10–100,*
*    the Publican must be able to kneel)*

A script could easily be written that would provide for actual verbal exchange between the sinner and Publican. However, from this author's experience with this skit, it comes across quite effectively with a narrator reading the passage directly from scripture while

*Both the Pharisee and the Publican go to the temple to pray. But, their prayers are quite different.*

the Publican and Pharisee "act out" the skit through effective body language.

In rehearsing this skit, it is important that the following be emphasized:

1. The Publican needs to practice mannerisms that would portray humbleness, meekness, and a sorrowful spirit.
2. The Pharisee, on the other hand, needs to practice the portrayal of arrogance and "lofty spirit."
3. They would benefit from rehearsing the skit several times as the narrator reads the scriptural passage to establish the most comfortable pace for this skit.

# PARABLE OF THE
# LOST SHEEP

◆ ◆ ◆

*Scriptural background: St. Matthew,*
*Chapter 18, and Luke, Chapter 15*
  *Cast of Characters:*
  *Narrator or Reader*
  *The farmer—an older child (age 13 and*
  *up)*
  *A herd of sheep, 6–8—children ages*
  *5–7 (must be compliant and able to*
  *follow directions)*

This story is beautifully retold in the children's book, *The Lost Sheep* (1986), by authors Nick Butterworth and Mick Inkpen.

25

Most Christian bookstores should have this book or could order it for you. The illustrations are priceless! Especially since younger children are involved, it would be wise to read the story a couple of times to them showing them the pictures in the book. It would also be beneficial for the skit to be practiced particularly to help the reader of the children's book establish the slower pace that is required for the acting out of the skit and also for the farmer to establish the movements as illustrated in the book.

It is strongly recommended or suggested that the skit end as it is illustrated in the last page of the book with all the sheep snuggled up to the farmer at the table. Party hats, balloons and party toys coming out of the bag and distributed among the sheep would be effective to convey God's rejoicing over the return of those who have strayed.

A very appropriate song to sing following this skit is, "Jesus Loves Me." Adults should join in singing it, as well.

# THE LOST SHEEP
# A POSTSCRIPT

Skits such as this one provides an atmosphere of cuteness, especially as we enjoy younger children performing. Yet, there is a profound message for all here.

For the children participating in this skit, there is that relentless and unconditional love from God that is demonstrated. They need to know that even though they were not the one chosen to be the lost sheep, a big fuss would have been made over them, too, had they been the lost sheep. Likewise, the celebration was held because all the other sheep were accounted for, not just the one who had strayed.

Those in the audience should not be taken for granted either. There may be lost sheep in the audience who need the message that this parable offers. There may even be a person in the audience who feels unloved by anyone, perhaps an individual feeling so alienated from the human race that life no longer offers meaning or purpose. Who knows? And, of course, others need this message just to reaffirm God's love and concern for them.

## Some Short But Power-Packed Parables

Pray preceding this performance for God's message to penetrate the lives of all persons gathered.

# EZEKIEL'S VISION
# The Valley of Dry
# Bones—An Overview

**◆ ◆ ◆**

The following vision of Ezekiel, which is found in the 37th Chapter of the Book of Ezekiel, makes for an excellent skit for teens, particularly for its choreography.

As director of this skit, you will need to sit down with the participants and talk about the meaning of this allegory.

The bones, dry and lifeless, represent the Nation of Israel at a time that the people had turned their back on God, had forsaken Him spiritually and even physically. They had become scattered by intermarrying outside their nationality, worshipping false gods, if any at all.

The bones coming together and acquiring flesh was God's work to reunite His chosen people, to begin the process of healing their backslidden condition.

As Ezekiel is commanded to prophesy to the "four winds" and breath comes into the bones, it is God "pouring out His Spirit on His people."

# EZEKIEL'S VISION
# A Parable

◆ ◆ ◆

*Scriptural background: Ezekiel, Chapter 37*
*Cast of Characters:*
    *Narrator*
    *God—A mature, serious looking*
    *individual*
    *Ezekiel*
    *Dry bones—6-10 teens*

This skit is best done as the scriptural passage is read. It would be wise to practice the skit numerous times as the narrator reads

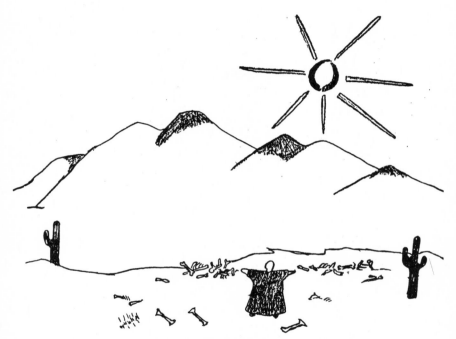

*Ezekiel's vision of the Valley of Dry Bones. The question is posed, "Can these bones live again?"*

the passage to acquire a comfortable timing between the reading and the actions.

The following sequence is suggested:

1.  Begin with the bones (teen players) coming out to the center of the room and forming various contorted positions, kneeling or stooped low to the floor, and remaining in statue position.
2.  Enter God with Ezekiel. God sends Ezekiel whirling into the midst of the bones and then Ezekiel walks in and around them (verse 2).
3.  As the reader reads verse 3, the person who is God comes in closer to Ezekiel. Even though he is not actually speaking, he holds both hands up majestically and faces Ezekiel at this time. (The idea is to show the audience, by actions, that God is conversing with Ezekiel.) The same goes for verse 4 as God gives Ezekiel the command to prophesy.
4.  In verses 5 and 6, Ezekiel keeps his eyes focused on God as he walks up to the bones and addresses them (all this time God needs to use gestures to let the

audience know He is talking to the bones.)

5. Then Ezekiel turns to the bones and prophesies. (Verses 7 and 8) He is startled by rattling and the sudden movement of the bones. One or two of the bones may want to have some type of rattling instrument to provide sound at this time. (If such effect is used, it should not be so visible as to detract from the skit.) In this same verse, the bones come together still kneeling or stooped low. But they are still dead. The bones have just attached themselves to each other.

6. In verses 9 and 10, God again speaks to Ezekiel commanding him to prophesy. The actions of God and Ezekiel are basically the same as for verse 3, but when God commands Ezekiel to prophecy to the four winds, Ezekiel should wave his hand in all directions as he beckons to the winds to bring back the breath of life to these bones. The bones stand to their feet as this part is read. (You may want to practice

all rising up together in unison or consecutively, one after the other in a prescribed order. Decide which works and looks best for your performance.) As verses 11–14 are read, the bones, now whole persons, continue moving as one unified group. It may be a dance or whatever lively (but civilized) movement decided upon by your group.

Your youth performers should enjoy doing this skit and perhaps may offer their own choreography to this performance. Director(s), be open to their ideas as long as the Biblical passage is made clear to the audience.

# THE FRIEND
# AT MIDNIGHT

*Scriptural background: Luke 11:5–10*
*Cast of Characters:*
    *Narrator*
    *2 neighbors at midnight: one in bed,*
    *the other "up and about."*

This parable, which teaches us the need for persistence in prayer, involves two individuals who play the part of next door neighbors.

Even though a lot of the skits in this book do not call for specific props and costumes, this one is most effective with them. Specifically, the two neighbors should be in pajamas with housecoats, house slippers, and, optional for comic effect, nightcaps. The neighbor who is "visited" at midnight should be lying down. (A small cot or fold up bed would be a suitable prop.)

As this parable from Luke is read slowly by a designated reader, the following sequence is suggested for two individuals (the neighbors) to pantomime:

>**Verse 5:** At midnight, one neighbor knocks at the imaginary door of his neighbor's house. He, or a person in the audience, could create the actual sound of knocking on a door. He pantomimes yelling through the closed door and holds up 3 fingers to show that he is requesting 3 loaves of bread.
>**Verse 6:** Continuing to yell through the closed door, he announces that the bread is for a friend who just arrived at his house and that he was not prepared to feed him. At this point, he holds an ear up to the door to listen for a response.
>**Verse 7:** (The man from his bed)— Following a big yawn, he motions for his neighbor to go away as he pan-

tomimes yelling his excuses at him for not getting out of bed.

**Verse 8:** The intruding neighbor starts to walk away but turns back and knocks again. The man then gets out of bed and comes to the door. With his hand out, and yawning, the neighbor hands him a loaf of bread (real or imaginary). Quickly the intruding neighbor gestures for a second loaf and then a third one. Of course, the good neighbor complies.

**Verses 9–10:** The narrator should read these verses to conclude this parable.

# SOME THOUGHTS TO SHARE

If time permits following this skit, it would be worthwhile sharing this parable's meaning. Of course, it tells us that persistence in prayer yields results. But, another aspect of this story involves what kind of things we ask for.

Three loaves of bread at midnight for a friend who has just arrived in town sounds a bit strange. But sometimes the things we ask of God may seem equally strange to Him who is "all-knowing" and Whose ways and thoughts are so much further removed from ours (Isaiah 55:8–9). Yet, because of His great love for us and understanding of our nature, He bestows on us even those things which seem as ridiculous as three loaves of bread at midnight.

# III

# TELEVISION
# AND
# TALK SHOWS

# WHAT'S "IN" ON
# TELEVISION?

◆ ◆ ◆

Outside of the afternoon soaps, probably the most common form of TV entertainment are TV talk shows which can be found on most stations at all times throughout the day and also in the evenings. What better way can interesting people and their unusual or distinct character be brought to the general public? And, of course, their high ratings contribute to the continuous rise of more such programs.

How much more insight could we have into the character and lives of great Bible personalities if we could bring them into the 20th century and have them appear on a TV talk show! With drama, this is possible.

A TV talk show skit setting such as is described in the introduction of this book is a great way of starting off an evening drama program.

# WHAT'S NEEDED?

People! People! People! You need a talk show host or hostess, guests (Bible celebrities), camera crew (more about it later), director and his/her assistant, make-up crew, and, of course, the TV audience.

# WHAT DO THEY DO?

The director and his/her assistant sit on director chairs or bar stools. The director leaves his/her seat merely to ask, "Ready on the set?" The assistant walks forward with a slate, counts down from 5 and gives it a click. (See Figure #1).

The camera crew enter the room about 4–5 minutes before the show is scheduled to begin, rolling a couple of carts loaded with

44

A.V. equipment and "heavy laden" with microphones, cords, lights, etc. All they have to do is "appear" as if they know what they're doing, i.e., connecting cords, testing equipment, setting up special lighting and sound systems. *Nothing really has to work*. It's all part of the act. Equipment can be old reel-to-reel tape recorders, TV's, record players, radios, anything with a lot of cords. Real headphone sets and a couple of lights are recommended. The camera crew should set up its equipment on a couple of tables already set up adjacent to and facing the set where the talk show is to take place.

The talk show host or hostess should be well-dressed for the part. They will have the questions to ask the guest in hand. (It is recommended for anxiety reduction for all involved that questions, at least most of them, be familiar to everyone actively involved in the talk show.) The questions should focus directly on the character of the person being interviewed. (See sample questions later.) Coming up with the questions need not be only one person's responsibility. They could come from a team of individuals who have familiarized themselves with the particular Bible character being interviewed, and especially by the individual who will be the Bible personality.

45

At this point, allow for some degree of flexibility and spontaneity to take place. Out of context from a question asked, the host or hostess of the show may come up with a new, unrehearsed question. Likewise, the guest may answer a question in a different manner than what was originally in his/her mind. This is what makes this such an exciting expression of art!

The guest or guests on the show serve in the most crucial role of the skit. The lights are focused on them and so are the eyes of the audience. For this very reason, keep encouraging them to loosen up, just feel the part and be themselves. Certainly this is easier said than done. But, it can happen . . . and it will.

It is not absolutely necessary for the guests to dress in costume. In fact, if the person is a surprise guest coming up on stage from out of the audience, they definitely should not be dressed in an unusual manner. But, if someone, say, is supposed to be "heavy with child," they should look it. If someone is supposed to be extremely old, it would help the audience to see them as the character they're playing if they would both look and act like an old person.

46

# TALK SHOW THEMES AND GUESTS

In this section, several "talk show" themes will be suggested. Those given as examples are certainly not an exhaustive list, only a suggestive one to get you thinking in this direction. Also, it is suggested that you think in terms of "professional" individuals in such areas as psychology, social work, education, law, and the medical profession to offer interpretive analysis and problem solving strategies, or whatever, to the subject being addressed. The "professional" individual need not be one in real life, and if not, should be knowledgeable enough in the area of "expertise" he/she is portraying to sound authentic.

Some suggested themes and individuals for them are the following:

1. Effects of becoming parents in later life:
   Abraham and Sarah, Elizabeth and Zacharias
2. Sibling jealously:
   Joseph and his brothers, The Prodigal Son, and his brother

3. People who have experienced sudden vocational changes:
   Jesus' Disciples
4. Very distinguished individuals:
   Jonah—experience from being inside a giant fish

# LONGEVITY OF LIFE
# An Interview with Methuselah

❖ ❖ ❖

*Scripture background: Genesis 5:21–27*
*Cast of Characters:*
   *TV set crew (as discussed in previous*
   *section)*
   *Talk show host or hostess*
   *Methuselah*

If you are interested in people who have lived the longest, the Bible is certainly our best resource.

Methuselah has been attributed with having lived to be the oldest man on record in the history of mankind. The scripture tells us his age at death was 965. Now, it would be interesting to hear from someone who has lived to be over 900 years of age, wouldn't it? Perhaps, it might be just as intriguing to hear from someone middle age when they have lived over 450 years. What kinds of questions might you ask this person in an interview? How about some questions dealing with some of these concerns?

1. The changing of history that he has already witnessed. His projections for the future that he thinks he'll live to see.
2. Mid-life concerns, i.e., goals, changes of emphasis (those things that were more important to him, but have since shifted, etc.).
3. Secret to his longevity of life.
4. His marital status: Presently widowed? Married? First wife? Second? . . . etc.

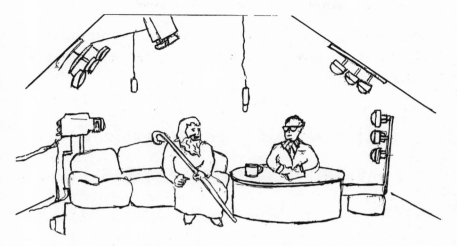

*Methuselah, at age 450, shares his
future life's goals on a T.V. talk show.*

See what kind of questions you can
come up with on the above aspects of his
life. Perhaps you can come up with more
concerns you would like to address in the interview.

# SIBLING RIVALRY: Guests from the Old and New Testament

## A TALK SHOW INTERVIEW

*Scripture background: First Family— Genesis Chapter 37 (Chapters 39–45 for further reading) and Second Family—St. Luke 15:11–32*

*Cast of Characters:*

*Talk show host or hostess*
*Joseph*
*3–4 of his brothers*
*Jacob (Joseph's father)*
*Other guests: The Prodigal Son, the Prodigal's brother, the father*
*Optional, but recommended: A psychologist/social worker or other therapist*

In way of introduction to this talk show episode, the host/hostess may wish to open with the point that, "Whereas most sibling rivalry falls within the norm for sibling relationships, at times such rivalry can result in extreme behavior and consequences such as in the case of the guests of this show today."

At this point, Joseph and several of his older brothers (there were 12 in all) could be introduced. Since there are several episodes of events taking place between Joseph and his brothers, perhaps it would be wise to cover just two or three of these, i.e., Joseph receiving his coat of many colors from their father, Jacob; Joseph's general attitude as he interprets his dreams; and perhaps his brothers' revenge as they decide to place him in a pit from where he is sold as a slave to the Egyptians. Questions asked could be focused on his brothers' growing hatred towards him, their father's role in contributing to some of those feelings, and how Joseph may have felt towards his brothers.

After this interview is completed, the talk show host/hostess should call in the next family; the Prodigal Son, his brother and their father. A little history from the Bible story can be told, either as part of the talk show host/hostess' introduction or by one of the members of this family.

Here lies the opportunity for the Prodigal's brother to really express his feelings over their father's treatment of the brother who just took off, leaving him with all the work that normally would have been shared by both. And, his blood pressure rises as he describes in detail the great welcoming home feast his father plans for the Prodigal brother.

The interview would not be complete without allowing the Prodigal himself an opportunity to express what was going through his mind that caused him to leave home in the first place. (This could best be expressed through a teen's driven need to get out on his own for the sake of independence from parental authority, to live out his own idea of what life on the "outside" should be like.)

Finally, the father should be allowed to express his reason for throwing a party for the son who left home and not acknowledging the other son for remaining home.

# STARTING A FAMILY IN THE LATER YEARS

*Scripture background: Genesis Chapters 15, 16, 17, 18, 21 and St. Luke 1:39–45, 57–80*
*Cast of Characters:*
 *Talk show host*
 *Abraham*
 *Sarah*
 *Hagar*
 *Ishmael (optional)*
 *Elizabeth*
 *Zacharias*
 *Psychologist*

It is suggested that the talk show host/hostess, Oprah or Sally Jesse Raphael, or whoever, give an introduction to the evening's (or morning's) program. This person may be sitting behind a desk or table (like Jay Leno's set up) or sitting in a special chair or even standing. Chairs should be provided up front for guests appearing on the show.

It's fine for the talk show host/hostess to have a script with questions to ask the guests (suggested types of questions are included on the next page). To make the guests more comfortable, it is a good idea to share these questions ahead of time with them. However, the guests should *not* have a script before them to read or memorize the questions or the answers. Doing so would detract from the spontaneity that should exist. A follow-up question to the guests *not* previously in the list of questions is not a reason for panic. Again, the guests should work at getting into "character" to the extent that they should feel at ease. It is often surprising to people participating in this kind of skit what neat one liner responses come from their lips during the actual show that they had not thought of when rehearsing.

A couple more comments are needed about this particular show. The audience will perk up when someone from in the audience, the individual playing Hagar, suddenly jumps up with a statement like, "I think I can answer that question much better and more honestly than those two!" (See question #2 below.) Having this person come forward as an unscheduled guest on the show will add an interesting dimension to the skit. (Just make sure there is an extra chair up front for her and her son, Ishmael, if he appears with her. Also, it is wise to introduce the second couple later in the skit. Have them join you after interviewing Abraham and Sarah. They will be an interesting couple because Elizabeth is still pregnant and must do all the talking. She might express some negative feelings about her pregnancy. Zacharias will be interesting to watch as he is trying to express himself although he can't talk!

Here are some questions that might be asked. Do not limit yourself to these. You may come up with better ones or additional ones, but don't overdo the questioning. Be aware of your obligation to the audience not to bore them. You can have a lot of fun with this skit.

Questions to Abraham and Sarah:

1. I understand you were told at a very old age that God would make a great nation from your family and yet you could not have a

child. What were your reactions to God's statement when He first said this to you?

2. Now let's see, I heard you had a plan to help make come to pass the prophecy that God had given to you. What was your plan? **(Hagar, Sarah's handmaid from the audience interrupts and comes forward to tell her part of the story.)

3. Well, Abraham and Sarah, it looks like you sort of took things into your own hands and created a problem for yourselves and for Hagar and her son. (Any comments from Abraham or Sarah would be appropriate here.)

4. Sarah, will you please tell us about the 3 strangers who paid a visit and what one of them said to you? How did you react to this special saying?

5. Obviously what God and one of the three visitors you entertained has come to pass. You now have a son of your own. What's his name?

6. Would you please share with us a little about how it feels to have a young child at such a mature age?
7. Finally, Abraham, what do you plan to do to help Hagar and her son, Ishmael?

Questions for Zacharias and Elizabeth (still expecting):

1. Zacharias and Elizabeth, I understand that you are in the process of undergoing a similar experience as Abraham and Sarah. (Response from Elizabeth and Zacharias.)
2. Which one of you were the first to hear good news?
3. Excuse me, but I'm curious about Zacharias' inability to speak. Elizabeth, will you explain? Was he always mute?
4. Zacharias, how are you explaining this situation? . . . that is, starting your family so late in life?
5. Have you selected a name for your child yet? (The answer at this point would be, "no," since Zacharias is still mute—see Luke 1:62–64.) However, Elizabeth and

Zacharias might throw out a few names at this time, but not "John." (Zacharias could gesture or sign to Elizabeth)

6. Most parents have some preconceived notion of what they would like to see their child become in adulthood. What would you like your child to become?

It would be a nice idea to have an analysis of this situation offered by a "guest" social worker or psychologist. This person could also offer some problem solving strategies to bring healing to each family member.

The questions asked the individuals in this interview need to be kept general so as to allow each family member the opportunity to express their side of the problem.

# SUDDEN VOCATIONAL CHANGES
## An Interview with Jesus' Disciples

*Scripture background: St. Matthew 4:18–22*
*and St. Matthew 9:9*
*Cast of Characters:*
   *Talk show host or hostess*
   *Fishermen—James, John, Peter,*
   *Andrew*
   *Matthew*
   *Tax collector*

As the host/hostess interviews these individuals, the emphasis will be on impact of sudden career changes including the following:

1. Possible impact on family (if not immediate, the extended family).
2. Feelings (good or bad) of leaving past vocation.
3. Emotional concerns around walking into a whole new line of work without a formal job description, work contract, or benefit package.
4. How their new job, as Jesus' close disciples, is going.
5. Advice to others facing sudden career changes, particularly for such a noble cause as today's guests.

Here, too, an expert on career changes could be introduced and allowed to offer some suggestions on how to prepare for and cope with these major changes in one's life.

# IV

# NEWS FLASHES
# FROM OUR
# ROVING
# REPORTER

# NOAH
# AND THE ARK

◆ ◆ ◆

*Scripture background: Genesis, Chapter 6*
*Cast of Characters:*
    *TV anchor*
    *News correspondent*
    *A crowd of people—5–8*
    *Noah*

The following is a suggestion for how this skit might go:

TV announcer—"Tonight we're hearing of a neighborhood uprising over an alleged eccentric old man who is constructing a thing called an 'Ark' in the neighborhood playground. He claims he is merely taking orders from his 'God.' We now take you by news satellite to East Side Heights where this newsbreaking story is unfolding. Our reporter, Bob Walker, is on the scene . . . "

At the other side of the room, a group of people (5–8 people) have been standing around Noah in a "freeze position" until a reporter with a microphone walks into their midst. At this point, the "crowd" moves into action protesting against Noah and his Ark. The reporter interviews randomly any of the 5–8 people as they are protesting Noah's contraption. Also, of course, equal time is given in questioning Noah.

To the skit director: The people selected as Noah's complaining neighbors might be asking for lines to say or how to act. Help lead them into their role by having them imagine how upset they would be if some type of development or event came into their neighborhood that would pose some type of threat, say to their home value or quality of life. Would a monstrous looking structure being built in the neighborhood playground affect them? If not, how about a pair of every

*Noah faces many unforseen problems in the building of the Ark. He is called on by a news reporter to share his difficulties on the air.*

kind of animal roving through their streets? They would probably be carrying signs of protest, perhaps raising their blood pressure a bit over a threat to their neighborhood. The reporter will not have to ask many questions to pick up the mood of the neighborhood.

As the reporter turns to Noah, a whole different set of problems surface. The reporter's responsibility is to ask questions that will make these problems known to the public eye. Some of the questions asked should lead Noah to express the following:

1. Problems obtaining a building permit to construct something totally unheard of.
2. Code violations cited by the building inspector when specific directions on the "how to" and "with what materials" were given to him by God.
3. Clashes with Humane Society over the care of the animals as they await their entrance onto the Ark.
4. The general ridicule of Noah and his family, particularly his children at school, over this whole "Ark thing" when it had never before

rained a drop up to this time!
5. How it would be transported to a water source when there was no water in that area.
6. His wife's perspective (from Noah) on all that is happening.

When the interview is finished, the interviewer should offer a summary or conclusive statement that would offer some type of closure to this news segment. He/she should then return the TV viewers back to the news anchor who can also offer a statement about this news flash and a "thank you" to the reporter on the scene. The skit might end with saying something like, "It's time for a commercial break but we'll be right back with some more exciting news as it's happening."

# THE TAKING
# OF JERICHO

*Scripture background: Joshua 6:1–20*
*Cast of Characters:*
   *Joshua*
   *Captain of the Israelite Army*
   *4 ark bearers (children age 7–9)*
   *4–6 trumpeters*
   *Marchers (more the merrier)*
   *2 Jericho wall guards (the enemy)*
   *On-site reporter/interviewer*

It is important that the seating of the audience, preferably in a sizable room, be somewhat prepared for an event of this magni-

70

tude. Make sure the aisles are kept clear and even though you don't want the element of surprise eliminated, you don't want to shock anyone into having a heart attack, either!

To prepare the participants for this skit, you may want to pass out a general handout such as the one on page 74, titled "The Taking of Jericho (A Sample Handout)." Also, for item #3 from this sample handout, you may want to pass out 3 × 5 cards with more specific cues written on them such as: "When you are interviewed by the reporter, you will have a positive outlook on what you are being commanded to do."

Another cue card given to another member of the marching army may call for an extremely negative attitude about this senseless marching, etc.

The interviewer should be equipped with a portable microphone and prepared to interview Joshua, the captain of the Israeli Army, a trumpet player or two (the opportunity for some real humor here), a couple of marchers and, of course, a couple of "look out men" on the other side of the wall. (Just imagine how silly the Israelites look walking around their wall totally unarmed!) The person guarding the wall can be prepared to offer the reporter their impressive list of weaponry (missiles, etc.) poised for use against any real threat to their city.

A possible sequence of events for this skit could be the following:

1. The Israelites march around the room once and then exit. In the following sequence: Joshua and the captain of the army, followed by trumpeters, the Ark of the covenant and the rest of the marchers. (The enemy will be positioned in the middle of the room, sitting on bar stools for visibility.) The wall can be imaginary as long as they (the enemy) raise up to address the reporter as though they are looking over the wall.

2. A second march into the room echoing their leader. (You might suggest that teens in your drama group develop a "sound off" for this skit). Half way around the room they are halted by the leader. At this point, Joshua and the captain are interviewed. Perhaps one or two of the marchers, as well, with other soldiers might

echo their sentiments to the person's comments.

3. Complete the march and exit the room.
4. The interviewer speaks to the enemy and gathers their viewpoint.
5. A third march around the "wall" interrupted by the interviewer who questions a couple of other marchers.
6. The march resumes. Just before leaving, Joshua commands the marchers to halt. The trumpeters position their imaginary trumpets and pretend to blow them. *All* the marchers place their hands at the side of their mouths to "give a great shout" (a silent shout, please). All *eyes,* which are *raised slowly, are lowered,* as if watching a great wall tumble down to the ground! The audience will know what is happening at this point only by these stressed actions being followed.
7. The march resumes as the army marches out of the room.

The reporter makes a statement and then returns the audience to the New's anchor person.

NOTE: From this author's experience directing this skit, there is a need to offer additional support to the adults participating as marchers because of their embarrassment at marching around the room.

The following is a suggestive handout you may want to consider giving to those individuals involved in the skit when you have recruited them. A similar type handout could be presented to participants in other skits in this book. The more information you can offer, without taking away from participant's spontaneity and creativity in responses, the more comfortable they should feel in participating in this and other skits.

# THE TAKING OF JERICHO (A SAMPLE HANDOUT)

You have been selected to participate in a skit demonstrating this supernatural event. Thank you very much for your willingness to participate.

First of all, you will enjoy this experience. Relax. Even though we will be telling a
Biblical story, we can have a lot of fun with
this skit at the same time.

There are a couple of things you can do
to prepare for this skit which are as follows:

1. Mark the date on your calendar so
   you'll remember when to be
   there.
2. Read Joshua 6:1–20 to get the
   Biblical account of this story.
3. Think about this famous battle.
   Place yourself in the position of
   the Israelites as they marched day
   after day around the walled city of
   Jericho. What might your thoughts
   be? Would you consider mutiny
   against the leader? How about the
   mental state of Joshua? Could he
   be the victim of sunstroke and in
   need of help? . . . Or perhaps you
   see this event and your participa-
   tion in it as the extension of God's
   hand. You may see this as a test
   of faith for you personally. But,
   whatever type of thinking you
   choose to represent, be willing to
   express it if by chance you are

asked by a news reporter on the scene.

4. Just follow the leader. Joshua will be leading you around Memorial Hall (encircling the Wall of Jericho). You'll be in a group of marchers. First will be the trumpeters, next the Ark of the covenant, and then the rest of you. Echo back what Joshua yells in the march.

5. No costumes are needed. Just be yourself (with some humor).

# THE MIRACLE AT THE POOL OF BETHESDA

*Scripture background: St. John 5:1–9*
*Cast of Characters:*
 *5–6 individuals representing the*
 *disabled (one, the impotent man of 38*
 *years)*
 *A roving reporter (with microphone)*
 *Jesus*
 *Anchor newsman/woman*

An excellent way of presenting this event is through the reporter interview with the disabled individuals gathered around the Pool of Bethesda. Also, at the end of the interview, a direct conversation between Jesus and one of the disabled at the pool would make this event complete.

77

## News Flashes From Our Roving Reporter

For most skits, it's suggested that there should be few, if any, props as well as character dress-ups. However, for this skit, a child's wading pool (no water necessary) would provide an excellent center of focus. The disabled individuals should look disabled. That is, people with eye patches, bandages, traction-like apparatus, wheelchairs, cots, will help portray the setting. Everyone should be in their places before the skit starts. The following is a suggested sequence for this skit:

1. The news anchor person from the reporting desk announces that, "An alleged body of water known as the Pool of Bethesda is said to possess some magical source of healing to certain individuals as they dive into its waters. By satellite cameras, we take you live to this mysterious Pool of Bethesda where our reporter, (name), will speak to those people gathered awaiting their time of healing from this special water."

2. The reporter identifies himself and the station he is from then begins interviewing the people around the pool. His questions would

focus on specifics of the person's disabilities, what they have heard or witnessed around the pool, how they found this place, etc. (It would be nice to have one person who has claimed they were healed in the water.) For time's sake, he/she probably would not want to ask each person more than a few questions. What should come across in this interview session is the people's frustration in waiting for their turn to get into the water.

The reporter then offers a summary statement to TV viewers and leaves the scene.

Jesus now enters, and seeks out the person who has been at the Pool of Bethesda for 38 years. This part of the skit should come directly out of the scripture where this man's healing is recorded. It is important that Jesus asks him if he wants to be healed. This is a very important element to this event.

Following the man's healing by Jesus, the skit is ended and everyone should abandon the wading pool area.

Some follow-up discussion questions:

1. What might have been the "magical element" in the Pool of Bethesda that healed certain people?
2. Why do you suppose Jesus asked this particular gentleman if he wanted to be healed?
3. Why didn't Jesus heal everyone who was lingering around this pool?

# V

# THE SCRIPTED SKITS

# THE TRUE GOD
# CONTEST

◆ ◆ ◆

*This skit, taken from I Kings 18:15–40, is written as a scripted play with the following parts:*

    *Narrator (all parts with the Roman numeral III)*

    *The "Wicked King Ahab"*

    *Elijah, the Prophet*

    *Israelites 1 and 2 (spectators in the crowd)*

    *Some false prophets (3–4 people)*

    *Ahab's servants (2 people)*

    *Leaders of Israel (2 people)*

## The Scripted Skits

The play is also written in such a way that it could be read by three narrators in its entirety as members of the cast pantomime the action. If this is done, it is suggested that the reading be divided by characters in the following way:

| Narrator I | Narrator II |
|---|---|
| Elijah | Ahab |
| Israelite 1 | Israelite 2 |
| Prophets of Baal | |
| (read by one person if pantomimed) | |

All parts designated with the Roman numeral "III narrator" would be read by the third narrator.

No props are needed. However, a certain area of the performance area should be designated as the fire pit area (the altar for sacrifice). This is the focal point of the skit's setting.

Narrator III: Our story picks up with an arranged meeting between the prophet, Elijah, and the wicked King Ahab of Israel. The two of them have long disagreed as to who the true God is. You see, King Ahab has a

84

thing going with the false gods of Baal and is leading the Israelites into this false worship. Of course, Elijah is a bit sore over this because he knows that God Jehovah is the one true God. It is Elijah's God that longs for Israel to choose Him as their God.

III. As Ahab spots Elijah in the crowd, he yells out to him,

II. "Oh, there you are, you scoundrel. I've been waiting for some time to kill you. I've had just about enough of this God Jehovah thing. You are confusing all my subjects. Here I've worked long and hard to get all these Baal images up throughout the land, not to mention the expense of carrying out such a mammoth project. And, now you dare to subvert the people to believe in your God! Pooh, pooh, Elijah, yours is only one God. Mine are many."

III. In reply to Ahab's insulting remarks Elijah responds,

II. "Oh, don't take it so hard your majesty, oh King. It is not me but you who is turning away from the one true God who I serve and who I urge all of Israel to turn back to worshipping. I'll tell you what to do your majesty, or rather suggest that you do. Send all the people of Israel to meet us at Mount Carmel at sundown. And, . . . oh, gather your 450 prophets of Baal to meet there also."

III. All the people of Israel gradually move towards the Mount, but not without a lot of murmuring and complaining. What could the purpose of another such gathering be? Usually such meetings are for the purpose of listening to King Ahab. And well . . . he is not the most interesting person to listen to. But, this time it is not King Ahab standing at the podium, but Elijah. What a pleasant surprise.

After Elijah clears his throat, he begins his speech,

I. "Okay, folks, I don't mind telling you I'm a little perturbed by your wishy washy, lax attitude about whose God you're worshipping. It's time to make a definite decision."

III. Two Israelites in the crowd begin chattering,

I—Israelite 1. "What in the world could he possibly be talking about?"

II—Israelite 2. "Who knows? He could be delirious from being in the sun too long. And, besides, I hear that Queen Jezebel has been out to get him. Perhaps this, too, has started to affect his thinking."

I—Israelite 1. "Well, let's hear him out. His speech has got to be better than anything we would hear from his majesty, King Ahab."

III. Elijah, overhearing the muttering in the crowd continues,

I. "Come on folks. You know what I'm talking about. One day you're worshipping one of the gods of Baal and the next day another. And, only when Israel is in a real bind do you even consider the real God, Jehovah."

III. The two Israelites in the crowd resume their conversation,

I—Israelite 1. "Come on now. We're not all that bad, Elijah."

III. In disgust, King Ahab yells over to Elijah,

II. "All right, Elijah. We've heard just about enough of your subversive speech. Come now servants, seize him and cut off his head."

III. Gesturing to Ahab's servants to back off, Elijah continues,

I. "Now wait a minute. Oh King, allow me to engage my God in a contest against your gods of Baal to see which god or gods is or are real. If my God loses the contest, you can take my life. Is it a deal?"

III. Ahab stalls for a minute, then replies,

II. "Well . . . I . . . I don't know . . . I . . . "

III. Elijah breaking in says,

I. "What's the big deal, oh King? There's a new saying out that goes something like this, "Put up or shut up. No offense, oh mighty King. What is your answer?"

III. Ahab, responding in both disgust and embarrassment at having been drawn into this defensive position, replies,

II. "Oh, alright, Elijah. Let's get it over. I have much more pressing matters to deal with.

Now, what's the nature of this . . . this contest that you're proposing?"

III. Anxious to get on with the contest, Elijah says,

I. "King, command your false prophets to bring us two bulls, one for themselves and one for me. Have your servants prepare the bulls for sacrifice. We'll set up an altar for each of us. Here, I'll set mine up on this spot. You can have that area over there, your majesty. Now, oh King of Israel, my plan is for you to have your false prophets call on the gods of Baal to light your sacrifice and I will appeal to my God to do the same to my sacrifice. And, the God who answers by lighting the sacrifice will be the God that we'll all worship and serve, okay?"

III. Everyone at the gathering from both sides agrees to the deal offered by Elijah. So the servants, prophets and Elijah set to work preparing for the sacrifices. The people of Israel make themselves comfortable as they anxiously wait for the contest to begin.

Then the prophets of Baal begin calling on their gods,

*The Scripted Skits*

I—Prophets of Baal (in unison). "Oh Baal, hear us. Oh Baal, hear us. Oh Baal, light our fire. Oh Baal, gods of all gods, hear our plea. Light our fire."

III. They continued their calling and pleading from sun up to sundown. They even began jumping up and down on their altar as they called out to Baal. But, nothing happened.

III. Then, one Israelite turns to another,

I—Israelite 1. "Quite a show, wouldn't you say?"

III. Another Israelite in the crowd yells out in reply,

II—Israelite 2. "A show? You've got to be kidding! It's a good thing I didn't make any plans for today. Otherwise, I'd feel guilty sitting around all day watching nothing!"

III. Elijah bellows out to the Prophets of Baal,

I. "Hey, guys, you've got to holler a little louder. I don't think your god heard you. Maybe the batteries need replacing in his hearing aid. Ha! Ha! Perhaps he's busy con-

90

versing with one of his colleagues. I'm sure he doesn't appreciate being interrupted. Or, perhaps he's in the lavatory. He should be coming out shortly! Oh, I know. He left on a business trip. But he'll return . . . sometime in the future."

III. And so, the entire day passes and there's no response from the false prophet's and Ahab's gods. It's now getting on to sundown and time for the evening sacrifice. It's now time for Elijah's part of the contest to begin. Elijah built his altar using twelve stones, each representing a tribe of Israel. Around the circle of stones, he dug a trench and on the altar he placed the sacrifice.

After finishing the preparation of the altar and the sacrifice, Elijah stands before his audience,

I—Elijah. "Now folks, move this way and witness what the true god of Heaven and Earth will do. Whoops . . . I almost forgot. (Gesturing to Ahab's servants.) Hey you and you and you, bring some buckets of water, four buckets for starters."

III. So Elijah continues pouring water over the altar as the buckets are brought to him.

## The Scripted Skits

Elijah then calls out for more buckets of water,

I—Elijah. "Bring them on, boys. Keep them coming. Let's get this altar wet!"

III. Annoyed at watching Elijah pour the water over the altar, one Israelite says to another,

I—Israelite 1. "Why didn't he just dig a well next to the altar and pump it?"

III. The Israelite next to him in reply says,

II—Israelite 2. "I don't know. I bet this is just a stalling technique. I saw it once in an old John Wayne film."

III. In spite of the negative comments coming from the crowd, Elijah makes his request to God,

I—Elijah. "Hear me, oh Lord God Jehovah, as I call on you this evening. Your people of Israel are gathered here. They need to know that you are the one true God that they should worship. Grant to your people a sign of your power by providing the fire for this sacrifice. Surely the hearts of your people will again be turned towards you."

III. The fire of the Lord fell from the heavens consuming the sacrifice, even singeing the stones around the altar.

Everyone witnessing this sight kneeled and began worshipping God saying, "The Lord, He is God. The Lord, He is God."

Elijah gesturing to some leaders of Israel commanded,

I—Elijah. "Take hold of the prophets of Baal and don't let any get away. Today, the power of God has been revealed to Israel."

III. Elijah has won the contest. The false prophets were taken to a brook named Kishon and executed. The people turned back to the true God for awhile. As for Ahab . . . well, that's another story for a later time.

The End

# THE RESURRECTION OF LAZARUS

*This skit, taken from St. John 38–44, is written as a* scripted play *with the following parts:*

> *Mary*
> *Martha*
> *Lazarus*
> *Jesus*
> *Servant (messenger)*
> *2 or 3 disciples*
> *Narrator*
> *3–4 audience participants*

**S**etting: There are three settings, one is at the home of Mary, Martha, and Lazarus; another at the village where Jesus and his disciples are staying; and the third is at the cemetery. Like other skits in this book, there is not a vital need for a formal stage set up with scenery or backdrop. A couple of chairs at center stage for Mary and Martha, a cot for Lazarus, a chair for Jesus at the side of the room or stage is sufficient (His disciples could kneel around Jesus or stand as long as they don't block Him from the audience's view).

Scene 1—Home of Mary, Martha, and Lazarus. Lazarus is lying on the cot (some moaning). Mary is seated knitting, reading a book, or whatever. Martha is pacing the floor.

Martha: "I've had it up to here, Mary! (Hand placed across her forehead.) I don't mind Jesus coming over for Sunday dinner, He and those disciples of His, but where is He when you need Him?" (Gestures for servant.) "Sheldon, go now and inquire where Jesus is. When you find Him, tell Him we need Him immediately. Lazarus is getting weaker by the hour. I'm sure Jesus could heal him if He were here. Do hurry now."

Servant runs over to individuals in the audience inquiring as to the whereabouts of Jesus and His disciples. (Perhaps these individuals should be warned ahead of time that they will be used in this manner. Several will shrug their shoulders and nod their heads "no." The last person will get out of their seat and direct the servant to where Jesus is seated talking to His disciples.)

Jesus to His disciples: "Now when you go out to share the good news, go out two by two and carry nothing . . . " interrupted by servant (a cough).

Servant: "Beg your par . . . par . . . don, Sir." Hate to interrupt. Miss Martha and Miss Mary begs your attendance at their home now. Lazarus is sick. He's real sick, Sir. Can you come? They want you now."

Jesus to servant: "Calm down now, my young man. Tell them I'll come. Thanks for the message." (Sends servant back.)

Jesus to His disciples: "Now. Let's see. Where was I . . . Oh, yes . . . Go forth two by two and carry neither purse or change of clothes . . . "

John (interrupting): "Master, why do you tarry here with us? Lazarus has need of you immediately." (The other disciples agreeing with John begin murmuring.)

Jesus (calming His disciples): "All in good time, men. All in good time. I can assure you that our friend, Lazarus, is okay, just sleeping. He will fully recover."

Back at Mary and Martha's house three days later. The servant has just returned from delivering his message. He is out of breath from rushing back.

Servant to Mary and Martha: "Is Jesus here? Is Lazarus okay?"

Martha: "Have you not heard, Sheldon? Our brother, Lazarus, is dead. He died soon after you left to find Jesus. Did you not see Jesus? I can't wait to have a few good words with Him. Well, did you or did you not see Him, Sheldon?"

Mary: "Easy now, Martha. Give him a chance to answer."

Servant: "Ah . . . yes, ma'am. I saw Him. He said He would soon come."

## The Scripted Skits

Mary: "I'm sure Jesus has a good reason for not getting here on time."

Martha (half weeping, yet angry): "I can't wait to hear His excuse."

Jesus and a couple of disciples enter.

Martha: "Where in the world have you been? If you had been here sooner, our brother and your friend would not have died!"

Jesus (attempting to calm her): "Have faith, Martha. Your brother, as I told Sheldon a few days ago, only sleeps. Do you not know that I have been granted the power to raise those who have died?"

Martha (again weeping): "I know . . . I know . . . But he is our brother. It's just so hard to believe."

Mary (walks over to Martha putting her arm around Martha): "It's okay, Martha. He's right, you know."

Jesus: "Take me to see where Lazarus lies that I can mourn my dear friend's passing."

# The Resurrection of Lazarus

Jesus is led away by Mary and Martha to where Lazarus is buried.

They come to the grave site of Lazarus.

Martha (to Jesus): "See. He's been buried in this tomb for 3 days. You surely realize it's too late to do anything."

Jesus, without a word, kneels before Lazarus' tomb and weeps. (He stops weeping when the narrator begins to read but remains frozen in the kneeling position during the reading.)

Narrator: "Jesus wept, but why? He knew He would raise Lazarus from the dead. So why should He weep? Was it for the mortality of human life? But, no. There is life beyond death for all who believe in Him. And Lazarus was such a believer. Could He have been reflecting on the hopelessness of mankind without His power to redeem and restore? Was it His own pending death that came to His mind as He looked on at Lazarus' tomb? Or was it more for all those people, particularly His closest friends who weren't sure of His power to raise the dead? More importantly, could it have been the doubting of who He was by those who He thought knew Him best?"

Jesus stands to His feet, arms outstretched and commands: "Lazarus, come forth!"

Lazarus slowly rises to his feet and comes over to Mary, Martha, and Jesus as all hug Lazarus. They all exit together.

The End.

# VI

# THE
# MONOLOGUE

# AN INTRODUCTION

◆ ◆ ◆

This type of skit is unique from the others in this book in three ways:

1. There is only one character in this skit (whence "mono" in mono-logue). He or she represents a specific Bible individual, a person-ality profile or, at the more spe-cific level, a single characteristic (i.e., a certain emotion, an atti-tude, a state of being, a personal-ity flaw, etc.) An example of each of the three types of monologues will be offered later in this chap-ter.

2. Acting is limited to accent in speech, if so desired, mannerisms, facial expressions and gestures.
3. The subject of the monologue generally focuses specifically on what the person is representing, i.e., if a Bible personality, the experiences and feelings of that individual who is being represented; if a personality type, specific expressions and examples of the personality type that is to be conveyed. If the person doing the monologue is representing a state of being, then specific descriptive terms should be incorporated to convey this message to the audience.

Biblical monologues may be serious or humorous in their delivery. A combination of both can be quite effective in capturing and holding the audience's attention.

Dressing in costume to fit a period (Biblical, if a person of that day) or to convey a certain mood or feeling is also an effective tool in conveying your intended message.

If the monologue is incorporated into a service or a program, you might be introduced as a special guest from the past if you are representing a Bible character, or as examples of the other types, Mr. or Mrs. Happiness, a man or woman called, "Humble", etc.

# CLEOPUS
# An Obscure Disciple

This author's favorite monologue character is Cleopus. Hardly anything is mentioned about Cleopus' personality or character in scripture. Perhaps it is the mysteriousness about Cleopus through lack of description that makes him so interesting. One can use his imagination and creativity to develop a profile of lesser mentioned individuals such as Cleopus.

The only mention of Cleopus in scripture, found in Luke 24, depicts him as any ordinary person walking down a road, in this case, the road to Emmaus. What is extraordinary is who joins him and another individual on the road. It was Jesus after his resurrection from the dead.

106

Several clues to Cleopus' personality are inferred by this author from the limited mention of him. First of all, he didn't recognize the Lord following His resurrection. He could have been made spiritually blind for that time and place, but this author feels that he was so overcome by his sense of loss over someone he had trusted in that his emotions just got the best of him. The Lord is dead and all hope is gone. How could the thought even cross his mind that Jesus would be raised from the dead, even though he may have witnessed Jesus raising others from the dead? We can see Cleopus as a broken man over such a great loss. Reality or his perception of reality had suppressed any degree of faith he previously had. The loss of the Lord in a sense was a loss of power from which he depended.

The brief mention of Cleopus in scripture identifies him as just one of the crowd who followed Jesus. It's very possible that he had witnessed many of the events that Jesus was a part of including his healing services, feeding of the multitudes, confrontations with the religious leaders of the day as well as others, but without any particular focus being directed his way. He could probably be likened unto the devoted but more autonomous parishioner in the pew on Sunday morning.

So, as you think about your monologue, it is suggested that you be prepared to relate briefly some specific events, i.e., the healing of Jarius' daughter, the feeding of the multitude of 5,000, throwing out the money changers in the temple, etc. as though you, Cleopus, had been in attendance at these events. But, be prepared to speak of these events as "one of the crowd."

Got the picture? Can you visualize yourself as Cleopus, the obscure disciple of Christ?

The story continues. As the gentlemen are invited into a home by this stranger (the risen Savior) for a meal and reveals himself to them in the breaking of bread, one can visualize Cleopus' excitement and expression of personal hope restored. And, as the Lord turns to Cleopus, personally offering him bread, it's just like sitting around the table with the original twelve disciples. What a privilege to be served by the Master around His table! What ecstasy and excitement one feels along with Cleopus at this time! An obscure disciple known personally by the Master.

If Cleopus is the character you portray in monologue, it is important that you feel what Cleopus must have felt, the feeling of great loss at Christ's passing, the restoration of hope as Christ is revealed, the feeling of being known personally by the Lord as you describe Him turning toward you and saying, "Here Cleopus, my friend, take, eat of this bread. It is my body which was given for you."

# THE PHARISEE

This monologue "type" is an example of a personality profile. As the monologue is presented, a number of stereotypical characteristics of this person should be detected by the audience, i.e., a lofty attitude, wealthiness, false piousness, highly educated, and very prejudice. The following scripture references should help you in "feeling the part":

- Jesus' attitude regarding these people: St. Matthew 3:7-9, St. Matthew 15:3-9, and St. Matthew 23 (entire chapter).
- The Pharisee's attitude toward Christ: St. Matthew 15:1-2.

Now, the following are leading statements that, hopefully, will be helpful in getting you through this monologue. (They are not intended for rote memorization, only as a skeletal framework from which to elaborate.):

- Have you ever noticed how differently we dress from those commoners? Let me tell you where we shop . . .
- Certainly you have noticed we cross to the other side of the street when we see one of those other kind coming. Perhaps I should enlighten you..
- We are much more religious than other people. Take, for instance, our practice of Sabbath observance. We . . .
- I'm sure you've noticed our neighborhoods. Quite common a distinction between ours and theirs (Jews and Christian.) Take, for instance, our . . .
- Yes, you might best describe us as an elite subculture in our own right. We stand out much further than average in other areas such as . . .
- What would God do if He hadn't created and set apart dedicated people like us to watch over other's spiritual and moral well being?

- Have you ever seen my family tree? My family tree traces me directly back to Abraham, God's own chosen person for special recognition and blessings, indeed even the recognized and official "Nation of Israel."

# MRS. GREEDY
# Alias Mrs. Greenback

This monologue titled, "Mrs. Greedy, Alias Mrs. Greenback" is an example of how a person can represent a single human characteristic, in this case, a human character flaw.

This author's image of Mrs. Greedy is that of an older but feisty lady who has accumulated a large wealth of ideas on how to get more for less at other's expense. She capitalizes on her appearance, the tacky way she dresses, her age and her fixed income as tools to accomplish her aim. Thanks to the classic, *A Christmas Carol*, by Charles Dickens, we have the male version "Scrooge" of this monologue. However, if a lady is not willing to play the role of Mrs. Greedy, an uninhibited gentleman dressed as Mrs. Greedy would knock the audience to the floor in laughter and would most assuredly get the point across.

Below are suggested ideas Mrs. Greedy may wish to share with her audience as she describes some of her "saving methods." The suggested ideas to share are not intended for rote memorization. You may select from these ideas and add more of your own. Have fun with this monologue skit while sending out a message to your audience at the same time.

# MRS. GREEDY
# "HER IDEAS"

1. Money goes in the sock—no money for bus fare.
2. Contributions—roll up a $1 bill with a strip of newspaper inside it and wrap with a rubber band to make it look like more.
3. Dress in older, cheaper clothes when going to the market.
4. Never pass up pennies lying on the sidewalk—put them in your bank where you can get interest.

Mrs. Greedy, alias "Mrs. Greenback"
gladly shares her strategies on how to
get more for less with any audience.
The audience must decide whether her
strategies are ethically and spiritually
sound.

**115**

5. When hiring youngsters to work for you, precount what you are going to pay: make sure it is a little less than what is to be paid out. Put the rest away. When paying, empty out your purse to show you don't have anymore. Better yet, pay them much less than they are worth, but tell them you're giving them the opportunity of experience.

6. Play up the fact that you can only pay out so much (less than the asking price) when making a purchase.

7. When using coupons in the store, get the cashier to look the other way while you get your coupons back. You can use them several times with this method. Think of what you can save!

8. Don't give to charities. Keep your money for yourself, and save, save, save and bank, bank, bank!

9. No tipping. Absolutely not. Never tip. Think of how much you can save by not leaving tips.

10. Never sell anything (garage or yard sale) for less than your ask-

ing price, even if it's not worth what you're asking. Think money, money, money. It's better for you to have the money than for others to get bargains.

11. When going through customs with valuables, here's a way you don't pay duty: The officer asks, "Anything in your baggage to claim?" Just give a chuckle (demonstrate to the audience) and say, "Of course. All the family's heirlooms, the china, crystal, flatware and buckets of diamonds." More than likely, if you look like I do, they'll just take one crosseyed look at you and wave you on. The money you don't pay for custom's duty means more money you'll have for you.

12. When going out for lunch, go late for the lunch buffet, but not too late to enjoy a nice lunch. Eat slowly and you'll be there when the dinner buffet is available. So, you can eat both lunch and dinner for the price of lunch. What a deal! And, don't forget to carry a larger purse, like the one

## The Monologue

I always carry. Stock up on some extras, like rolls and such for yet another meal.

# OTHER SUGGESTED MONOLOGUES

Of a specific Bible person:

1. Thomas, the doubter (St. John 20:24–29)
2. Book of Jonah (All 4 chapters)
3. Naaman, the leper (II Kings 5)
4. Zaacheus (St. Luke 19:1–10)
5. John the Baptist (St. Matthew 3)
6. King Herod The Great (St. Matthew 2)

Of a character personality "Profile":

1. The High Priest of Jesus' day
2. The Sadduces (Matthew 3:7, 16:6, Acts 4:1–3)

3. The Multitude, a Representative, observing the miracles, healings, etc. of Christ.
4. The Good Samaritan (Luke 10:30–37)
5. The Prodigal Son (St. Luke 15:11–32)
6. An Angel (use your imagination)

Of a "characteristic":

1. The Poor in Spirit (Matthew 5:3)
2. One of the "Fruits of the Spirit" (Galatians 5:22–23)
3. Spiritual blindness (Isaiah 59:10; Matthew 6:23, 15:4; II Corinthians 3:14, 4:4; I John 2:11)

# CLOSING REMARKS
## Some Suggestions to the Director

- Prayerfully consider which Biblical events you wish to develop and perform. And pray.
- Think about who to approach for specific "characters." Approach people individually. Pray about it.
- When approaching individuals for parts, be supportive and empathetic if they are anxious or unsure. You will need to develop a feel for when to further encourage them to participate or when it's best to back off. Perhaps they'll come to you at a later date to volunteer. Pray for their confidence.

- Inform your volunteer fully of what's happening: Are there specific lines to memorize? Is it totally improvisational, without rehearsals? (Warning—this could easily turn the novice off immediately.) Will there be rehearsals and when? Continue to offer reassurance, support and encouragement.

- Emphasize the importance of participants familiarizing themselves with the scriptural background for the skit. Give them the Biblical reference for it. Ask them to read it over and over to get a feel for the story and particularly for the role they will be assuming. Pray for their understanding of the story and of their role.

- Whether the skit is scripted or not, handing the participants 3 × 5 cards with specifics (or generalizations) to reflect on while thinking about their part is helpful and should reduce some of their anxiety. (Suggestions and examples of these cue cards are offered with some of the skits.)

Also, a helpful tool is a general letter similar to the sample following the skit titled "The Taking of Jericho." Such a letter offers the performers or players a total or overall glimpse at the "flavor" of the skit.

- Be open to "twists" that may occur only during the final performance of the skit itself. An example might be a child playing the role as an innkeeper in Bethlehem who is supposed to turn away Mary and Joseph. But in the performance, the child's conscience prohibits him from being able to turn them away. Remember, you have prayed for God's guidance to be on each player. In this interesting "twist," the audience still must decide what they would do if they were the innkeeper. The message remains intact even though it might mean the other players need to fall in quickly to this sudden turn of events. How interesting the story can become in these situations!

Hopefully, this book offers many ideas that will be useful for you and your drama group. Also, it is hoped that this book will

## Some Suggestions to the Director

help stimulate your thinking to create more skits that are not included within this printed text.